1 JOKE A DAY

366 JOKES TO READ WITH YOUR FAMILY

SELECTION, CREATION AND ADAPTATION:
BUBBLES BOOKS

DESIGN AND ILLUSTRATION:
SILVIA ROMA

TRANSLATION AND ADAPTATION:
RHYS WESTON

D1462861

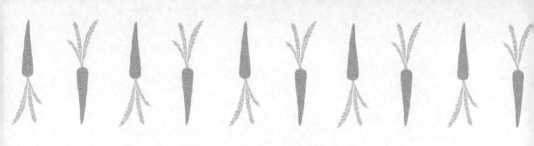

Welcome everyone!

THE SEASON OF LAUGHS WITH YOUR FAMILY HAS OFFICIALLY STARTED!

FROM THIS MOMENT ONWARDS YOU'LL HAVE A CHANCE TO SHARE A GOOD JOKE WITH YOUR FAMILY EVERY SINGLE DAY OF THE YEAR.

KIDS WILL BE THE ONES WHO LEAD THIS GREAT ADVENTURE! THEY'LL BE ABLE TO TELL SHORT, SIMPLE AND FUN JOKES WHILE PRACTISING READING AND DEVELOPING THEIR READING COMPREHENSION AND A SENSE OF HUMOUR.
ANY TIME IS A GOOD FOR A LAUGH WITH THIS BOOK; WHETHER HAVING BREAKFAST, ON A LONG CAR TRIP, AT YOUR GRANNY'S BIRTHDAY PARTY, OR IN YOUR BEDROOM WITH A SIBLING.

IF THERE'S NO ONE AROUND AT THE TIME TO SHARE THE JOKE, THAT'S FINE AS WELL! IT'LL MAKE YOU SMILE – AND YOU'LL BE ABLE TO TELL OTHER PEOPLE THE JOKES YOU'VE READ ANOTHER TIME.

LISTEN UP: BROTHERS AND SISTERS, GRANDPARENTS, MUMS AND DADS, AUNTS AND UNCLES, COUSINS, FRIENDS, CATS AND DOGS… THE FUN BEGINS HERE!

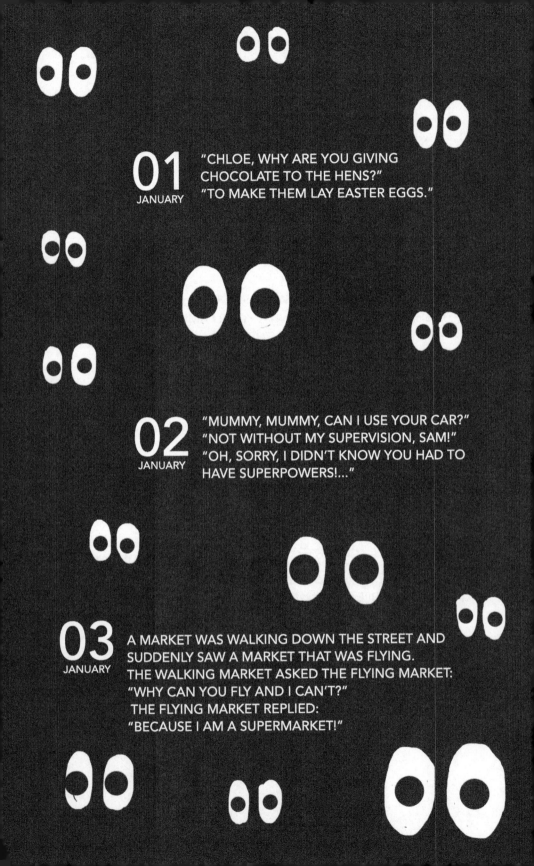

01
JANUARY

"CHLOE, WHY ARE YOU GIVING CHOCOLATE TO THE HENS?"
"TO MAKE THEM LAY EASTER EGGS."

02
JANUARY

"MUMMY, MUMMY, CAN I USE YOUR CAR?"
"NOT WITHOUT MY SUPERVISION, SAM!"
"OH, SORRY, I DIDN'T KNOW YOU HAD TO HAVE SUPERPOWERS!..."

03
JANUARY

A MARKET WAS WALKING DOWN THE STREET AND SUDDENLY SAW A MARKET THAT WAS FLYING. THE WALKING MARKET ASKED THE FLYING MARKET:
"WHY CAN YOU FLY AND I CAN'T?"
THE FLYING MARKET REPLIED:
"BECAUSE I AM A SUPERMARKET!"

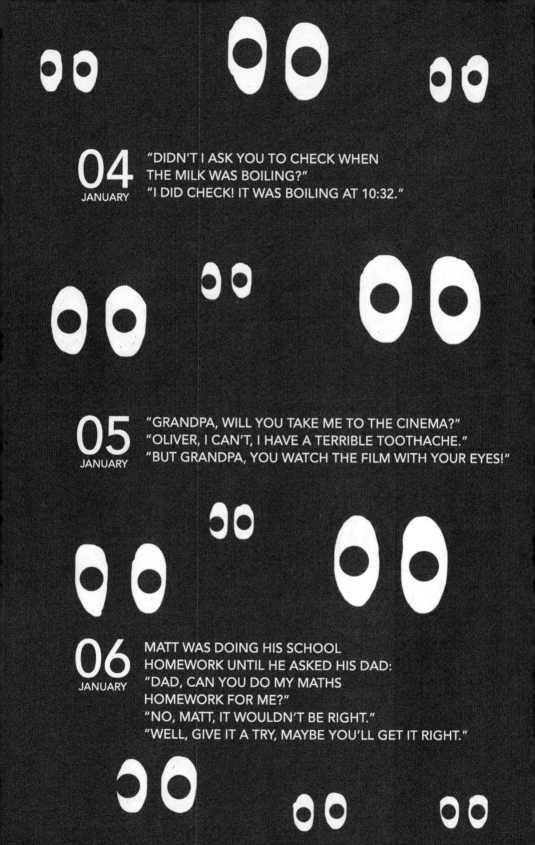

04
JANUARY

"DIDN'T I ASK YOU TO CHECK WHEN THE MILK WAS BOILING?"
"I DID CHECK! IT WAS BOILING AT 10:32."

05
JANUARY

"GRANDPA, WILL YOU TAKE ME TO THE CINEMA?"
"OLIVER, I CAN'T, I HAVE A TERRIBLE TOOTHACHE."
"BUT GRANDPA, YOU WATCH THE FILM WITH YOUR EYES!"

06
JANUARY

MATT WAS DOING HIS SCHOOL HOMEWORK UNTIL HE ASKED HIS DAD:
"DAD, CAN YOU DO MY MATHS HOMEWORK FOR ME?"
"NO, MATT, IT WOULDN'T BE RIGHT."
"WELL, GIVE IT A TRY, MAYBE YOU'LL GET IT RIGHT."

07
JANUARY

WHAT IS THE DIFFERENCE BETWEEN A FLY AND A BIRD? A BIRD CAN FLY BUT A FLY CAN'T BIRD!

08
JANUARY

"CHARLIE, COME TO THE KITCHEN QUICKLY, THE SPAGHETTI IS GETTING STUCK TOGETHER."
"DAD, I DON'T WANT TO GET INVOLVED, THAT SOUNDS LIKE A STICKY SITUATION!"

09
JANUARY

TWO LICE, FATHER AND SON, WERE WALKING ON A BALD MAN'S HEAD. THE FATHER SAYS TO HIS SON: "WHEN WE WERE YOUNGER, THIS USED TO BE A BEAUTIFUL FOREST!"

10
JANUARY

"HAVE YOU NOTICED THAT ALL YOU THINK ABOUT IS FOOD?" "B-COUS-COUS I LOVE IT!"

11
JANUARY

"DOCTOR, DOCTOR, AFTER THE OPERATION WILL I BE ABLE TO PLAY THE GUITAR?" "YES, OF COURSE, PERFECTLY!" "THAT'S SO COOL! BECAUSE I COULDN'T BEFORE."

12
JANUARY

WHY IS IT HARD TO HIRE A CLOWN? BECAUSE THEY HAVE BIG SHOES TO FILL!

13
JANUARY

WHAT TYPE OF MILK CAN
ONE GET FROM A SHORT COW?
CONDENSED MILK.

14
JANUARY

"DOCTOR, WHAT CAN I DO TO
KEEP ALL THE HAIR I HAVE LEFT?"
"IT'S QUITE SIMPLE, BY KEEPING
IT IN A LITTLE BOX."

15
JANUARY

WHAT DID ONE SLICE OF
BREAD SAY TO THE OTHER
BEFORE THE RACE?
YOU'RE TOAST!

16
JANUARY

"TIGERS, PANTHERS AND LIONS ARE HARMLESS ANIMALS, BUT PIGEONS, BIRDS AND CHICKS ARE DANGEROUS," SAID ONE EARTHWORM TO THE OTHER.

17
JANUARY

WHAT SHOULD YOU GIVE AN ELEPHANT WITH DIARRHOEA? SPACE, AND LOTS OF IT.

18
JANUARY

WHAT DID ONE FLIP-FLOP SAY TO THE OTHER? WE MAKE A GREAT PAIR!"

19
JANUARY

WHY DID THE CAPILLARY
LOVE TO LOOK AT
HIMSELF IN THE MIRROR?
HE WAS A LITTLE VEIN.

20
JANUARY

WHAT DID ONE FLEA SAY TO THE OTHER FLEA
WHEN THEY CAME OUT OF THE MOVIES?
SHOULD WE WALK HOME OR TAKE A DOG?

21
JANUARY

WHY DO PANDAS LIKE OLD MOVIES?
THEY'RE IN BLACK AND WHITE.

22 JANUARY

WHY ARE CATS GOOD AT
VIDEO GAMES?
BECAUSE THEY HAVE 7 LIVES.

23 JANUARY

WHY ARE SKELETONS AFRAID OF DOGS?
BECAUSE DOGS LOVE BONES.

24 JANUARY

ONE FISH SAYS TO THE OTHER:
"DID YOU KNOW THAT FISH ONLY
HAVE TWO SECONDS OF MEMORY?"
"WHAT DO YOU MEAN?"
"WHAT DO I MEAN ABOUT WHAT?"

25
JANUARY

WHAT DOES A 9 SAY TO
ANOTHER 9 WHEN HE SEES A 6?
LOOK AT THAT HANDSTAND!

26
JANUARY

WHY DID THE BANANA GO TO THE DOCTOR?
BECAUSE IT WASN'T PEELING WELL.

27
JANUARY

WHAT DID THE SNAKE SAY TO THE
NOISY CHILDREN AT THE LIBRARY?
SSSSSS

28
JANUARY

WHY DID THE INVISIBLE PERSON TURN DOWN A JOB OFFER? THEY JUST COULDN'T BE SEEN DOING IT.

29
JANUARY

HOW DOES A MOUSE FEEL AFTER TAKING SHOWER? SQUEAKY CLEAN!

30
JANUARY

WHAT IS THAT ANT DOING TWISTING A PIECE OF CHEWING GUM? THE CHEWING GUM TWIST.

31
JANUARY

WHAT DO YOU CALL A SKELETON
WHO WON'T WORK?
LAZY BONES!

01
FEBRUARY

EMILY ASKS HIS MOTHER:
"MUM, WHAT'S THAT IN YOUR
BELLY?"
AND SHE REPLIES:
"I HAVE A BABY WHICH WAS A GIVEN
TO ME BY YOUR DAD."
THE GIRL LOOKS AT HER IN FEAR
AND LOOKS FOR HIS FATHER TO SAY:
"DAD, DAD! DON'T GIVE MUM ANY
MORE BABIES, SHE'LL EAT THEM!!!!"

02
FEBRUARY

THERE WERE TWO TOMATOES IN THE FRIDGE:
"OH, I'M SO COLD!"
"OH MY, A TALKING TOMATO"

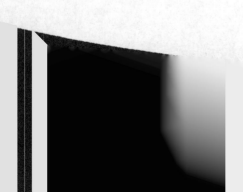

03
FEBRUARY

LIAM AND JO ARE WALKING DOWN
THE STREET AND LIAM ASKS:
"HOW DID YOUR EXAM GO?"
"REALLY TERRIBLE, I LEFT EVERYTHING
BLANK!"
"UH OH, THE TEACHER IS GOING TO
THINK WE COPIED EACH OTHER!"

04
FEBRUARY

WHAT DOES NUMBER 2 SAY
TO NUMBER 3?
DON'T HANG OUT WITH
NUMBER 1, HE ALWAYS
WANTS TO BE FIRST.

05
FEBRUARY

TWO FRIENDS ARE TRAVELLING ON
A TRAIN AND ONE SAYS TO THE
OTHER:
"HEY, HAVE YOU NOTICED HOW
QUICKLY THE TREES PASS BY?"
AND THE OTHER REPLIES:
"YES, ON THE WAY BACK WE
SHOULD GO BACK ON THE TREES."

06
FEBRUARY

BEFORE CROSSING THE STREET MR. OCTOPUS SAID TO HIS CHILDREN: "GIVE ME YOUR HAND, HAND, HAND, HAND, HAND, HAND, HAND, HAND."

07
FEBRUARY

"WHAT'S THE DIFFERENCE BETWEEN AN ELEPHANT AND A FLEA?"
"IT'S SIMPLE! THE ELEPHANT CAN HAVE FLEAS AND THE FLEA CAN'T HAVE ELEPHANTS."

08
FEBRUARY

MIA ARRIVES HOME FROM SCHOOL AND TELLS HER DAD: "DAD, DAD, I HAVE SOME GOOD NEWS AND SOME BAD NEWS!"
"TELL ME THE GOOD NEWS FIRST."
"I GOT A GRADE 9 IN MATHS!"
"AND WHAT'S THE BAD NEWS?"
"WELL, IT'S A LIE!"

09
FEBRUARY

MIA AND THOMAS CLIMB UP THE ROOF AND PLAY LEAPFROG FROM ONE HOUSE TO THE OTHER.
MIA JUMPS AND A TILE FALLS OFF. THE LADY BELOW ASKS:
"WHO IS UP THERE?"
MIA ANSWERS:
"MEOW, MEOW."
THE LADY CALMS DOWN. THEN THOMAS JUMPS UP AND ANOTHER TILE FALLS OFF.
THE LADY ASKS AGAIN:
"WHO'S UP THERE?"
TO WHICH THOMAS ANSWERS:
"JUST ANOTHER CAT."

10
FEBRUARY

DOCTOR, DOCTOR, I SWALLOWED A BONE.
-ARE YOU CHOKING?
-NO, I REALLY DID!

11
FEBRUARY

DURING A MATHS LESSON:
"LILLY, IF I HAVE 15 PEARS IN ONE HAND AND 10 IN THE OTHER, WHAT DO I HAVE?"
"HUGE HANDS, SIR."

12
FEBRUARY

DURING HISTORY CLASS, THE TEACHER ASKED WILLIAM:
"WHAT HAPPENED IN THE YEAR 1812?"
"HOW WOULD I KNOW, MISS? I WASN'T EVEN BORN THEN!"

13
FEBRUARY

WHY ARE RATS BAD AT TAKING PICTURES?
BECAUSE WHENEVER YOU SAY "CHEESE"
BEFORE TAKING THE PICTURE, THEY TRY
TO RUN OFF AND FIND IT!

.

14
FEBRUARY

"CHARLOTTE, DID YOU COPY JAMES'
TEST?"
CHARLOTTE, LOOKING INNOCENT AND
CONFUSED, REPLIES:
"NO, SIR!"
"THEN WHY ON QUESTION 3, WHERE
JAMES ANSWERED 'I DON'T KNOW', DID
YOU PUT 'ME NEITHER'?"

15
FEBRUARY

WHAT IS THE LAST LETTER OF THE ALPHABET?
"THE LETTER T"...
"YOU MEAN Z"!
"NO, MAN! OTHERWISE, IT WOULD BE ALPHABETZ".

16
FEBRUARY

THE TEACHER TELLS DAVID:
"ANSWER MY QUESTION RIGHT
NOW. WHAT IS 7 PLUS 2?"
DAVID REPLIES:
"RIGHT NOW."

17
FEBRUARY

THE TEACHER ASKS AMY:
"IS RICE WITH C OR S?"
AMY ANSWERS:
"HERE AT SCHOOL I DON'T
KNOW MISS, BUT AT HOME
IT'S WITH TOMATO."

18
FEBRUARY

SOPHIE'S MUM SAYS TO HER:
"NOW YOU BE GOOD TODAY! EVERY
TIME YOU DO SOMETHING BAD I
GET A GREY HAIR."
"AHHH, THEN YOU MUST HAVE
BEEN REALLY NAUGHTY! JUST LOOK
AT GRANDMA'S HAIR."

19
FEBRUARY

THE MATH TEACHER ASKS MIA IN CLASS:
"MAX, IF YOU HAVE 10 POUNDS IN ONE
POCKET AND IN THE OTHER YOU HAVE
TWO 100 POUND NOTES, HOW MUCH
DO YOU HAVE IN TOTAL?"
"SOMEONE ELSE'S TROUSERS, SIR."

20
FEBRUARY

"EVELYN, WHAT CAN YOU TELL
ME ABOUT THE DEATH OF
CHRISTOPHER COLUMBUS?"
"THAT I'M VERY SORRY, MISS."

21
FEBRUARY

"DID YOU KNOW THAT MY BROTHER HAS BEEN RIDING A BICYCLE SINCE HE WAS FOUR YEARS OLD?"
"OH YEAH? WELL, HE MUST BE A LONG WAY AWAY BY NOW..."

22
FEBRUARY

"TEACHER, WOULD YOU GET ANGRY WITH ME FOR SOMETHING I DIDN'T DO?"
"NO, KATE, OF COURSE NOT!"
"PHEW, BECAUSE I DIDN'T DO TODAY'S HOMEWORK."

23
FEBRUARY

WHAT HAPPENS IF A TREE FALLS INTO MUD?
"IT 'LEAVES' AN IMPRESSION!"

24
FEBRUARY

AT SCHOOL THE TEACHER
ASKS MATT:
"TELL ME MATT, WHAT YOUR
PERFECT SCHOOL BE LIKE?"
"CLOSED, MISS!"

25
FEBRUARY

"DO YOU WANT THE PIZZA
CUT INTO 6 OR 8 SLICES?"
"INTO 6 SLICES, PLEASE. I
DON'T THINK I CAN EAT 8."

26
FEBRUARY

WHAT IS THE WORLD'S
TALLEST BUILDING?
THE LIBRARY! BECAUSE IT
HAS THE MOST STORIES.

27
FEBRUARY

WHO HAS THE MOST TEETH?
THE TOOTH FAIRY.

28
FEBRUARY

ONE MOSQUITO WARNS THE OTHERS:
"BE VERY CAREFUL WITH HUMANS! THEY
ALWAYS WANT TO KILL US."
ONE OF THEM REPLIES:
"THAT'S NOT TRUE! THE OTHER DAY A
HUMAN WAS APPLAUDING ME."

29
FEBRUARY

"MUM, PLEASE STOP IT, I'M NOT GOING
TO SCHOOL TODAY!"
"GEORGE, YOU HAVE TO GO, IT'S YOUR
DUTY."
"MUM, GIVE ME ONE GOOD REASON
WHY I HAVE TO GO TO SCHOOL TODAY."
"BECAUSE YOU ARE THE HEADMASTER."

01
MARCH

WHAT'S BETWEEN
EARTH AND THE PLANETS?
LOTS OF SPACE!

02
MARCH

TODAY A MAN KNOCKED ON MY DOOR
AND ASKED FOR A SMALL DONATION
TOWARDS THE LOCAL SWIMMING
POOL... I GAVE HIM A GLASS OF WATER.

03
MARCH

WHAT WOULD HAPPEN IF THE
PLANET EARTH WERE A CUBE?
WE WOULD ALL BE CUBANS!

04
MARCH

A BIRD SITTING IN THE TREE ASKS:
"HEY, BEAR, WHY ARE YOU UP IN THIS TREE?"
THE BEAR REPLIES:
"I CAME UP HERE TO EAT APPLES."
"BUT BEAR, THIS ISN'T AN APPLE TREE. THERE
ARE NO APPLES UP HERE."
"IT'S OK, I BROUGHT MY OWN WITH ME."

05
MARCH

A MAN KNOCKS ON THE DOOR.
"WHO'S THERE?"
"BOO."
"BOO WHO?"
"DON'T CRY, IT'S JUST A JOKE."

06
MARCH

WHY ARE WORMS CONSIDERED
TO BE GREAT COMPANY?
BECAUSE THEY ARE ALWAYS
DOWN TO EARTH

07
MARCH

WHY DID THE CANDLES
QUIT THEIR JOB?
THEY WERE ALL TOO
BURNT OUT.

08
MARCH

"I WOULD LIKE TO LIVE
ON A DESERT ISLAND."
"ME TOO."
"OH GREAT, IT HAS ALREADY
STARTED TO FILL UP THEN!"

09
MARCH

WHAT DOES A TRAFFIC LIGHT SAY TO THE OTHER?
STOP LOOKING AT ME! I'M CHANGING.

10
MARCH

CHARLOTTE SAID TO HER MATH TEACHER:
"TO SHOW YOU HOW GOOD I AM
AT FRACTIONS, I ONLY DID HALF MY
HOMEWORK!"

11
MARCH

WHAT DOES ONE WALL SAY TO
ANOTHER WALL?
I'LL MEET YOU AT THE CORNER.

12
MARCH

WHY DOES CHLOE BRING GLUE
TO THE RESTAURANT?
IN CASE SHE BREAKS HER DIET.

13
MARCH

WHY DID PEOPLE STOP GOING TO THE LIBRARY?
BECAUSE THEY HEARD IT WAS ALL BOOKED!

14
MARCH

WHY DO WHITE STORKS SLEEP WITH
ONE LEG TUCKED UP?
BECAUSE IF THEY TUCKED BOTH OF
THEM UP, THEY WOULD FALL OVER.

15
MARCH

ON A FIELD TRIP, THE TEACHER TELLS JESS:
"DON'T GO NEAR THE LION'S CAGE! "
TO WHICH JESS REPLIES:
"DON'T WORRY, MISS, I'M NOT GOING TO
DO ANYTHING TO IT."

16
MARCH

WHAT REPTILE DO YOU GET
WHEN YOU CROSS A LION
WITH A CAMEL?
A CHAMELEON!

17
MARCH

ON A FIELD TRIP, THE TEACHER TELLS JESS:
"DON'T GO NEAR THE LION'S CAGE!"
TO WHICH JESS REPLIES:
"DON'T WORRY, MISS, I'M NOT GOING TO
DO ANYTHING TO IT."

18
MARCH

WHAT ANIMAL CAN JUMP HIGHER THAN A HOUSE?
ANY, BECAUSE HOUSES CAN'T JUMP.

19
MARCH

WHAT IS THE TOMATO'S
FAVOURITE DANCE?
SALSA!

20
MARCH

THE CHILD ASKS HIS MOTHER:
"MUM, WHAT DAY WAS I BORN?"
"AUGUST 20TH."
"WHAT A COINCIDENCE, I WAS BORN ON
THE SAME DAY AS MY BIRTHDAY!"

21
MARCH

A BOY TELLS HIS FATHER:
"DAD, DAD, AT SCHOOL THEY CALL ME
SELF-SERVING."
"WHY DO THEY CALL YOU THAT, SON?"
"GIVE ME A POUND AND I'LL TELL YOU."

22
MARCH

HOW DO TWO FLOWERS GREET EACH OTHER? HEY BUD, HOW'S IT GROWING?

23
MARCH

"MUM, MUM, I ALMOST GOT AN A TODAY."
"VERY GOOD, SOPHIE! BUT... WHY ALMOST?"
"BECAUSE THEY GAVE IT TO THE GIRL NEXT TO ME."

24
MARCH

WHAT DID THE BALLOON SAY TO ANOTHER BALLOON? BE CAREFUL WITH THE CACTUSSSSSSSSSSSSSSS

25
MARCH
WHY DON'T LADYBIRDS PLAY HIDE AND SEEK?
THEY ALWAYS GET SPOTTED!

26
MARCH
WHICH SCHOOL SUPPLY IS THE KING OF THE CLASSROOM?
A RULER!

27
MARCH
WHY DOES THE MUSIC TEACHER NEED A LADDER?
TO REACH THE HIGH NOTES.

28
MARCH

WHAT DID ONE FISH SAY TO THE OTHER?
KEEP YOUR MOUTH SHUT AND YOU'LL
NEVER GET CAUGHT.

29
MARCH

WHY DID THE ORANGE STOP IN
THE MIDDLE OF THE ROAD??
BECAUSE IT RAN OUT OF JUICE.

30
MARCH

A SNAKE ASKS ITS MOTHER:
"MOM, ARE WE POISONOUS?"
"WHY DO YOU ASK?"
"BECAUSE I BIT MY TONGUE."

31
MARCH

WHAT HAPPENS WHEN YOU TALK TO A COW? IT GOES IN ONE EAR AND OUT THE UDDER!

01
APRIL

"AREN'T YOU GOING TO WATER THE GARDEN?" "BUT IT'S RAINING." "WELL, TAKE THE UMBRELLA THEN."

02
APRIL

TWO TRIANGLES ARE WALKING DOWN THE STREET AND SEE THE LETTER CAPITAL A. ONE OF THE TRIANGLES SAYS: "LOOK AT THAT TRENDY GUY, HE'S WEARING A BELT!"

03
APRIL

THE HISTORY TEACHER ASKED JO:
"WHERE WAS THE FRENCH PEACE
TREATY OF 1800 SIGNED?"
JO REPLIED:
"ON A PIECE OF PAPER, SIR."

04
APRIL

THE TEACHER ASKED THE PUPILS TO DRAW A COW
GRAZING IN A MEADOW. WITHIN SECONDS, NOAH
PUT UP HIS HAND AND HANDED HER A BLANK
SHEET OF PAPER.
"YOU HAVEN'T DRAWN ANYTHING", THE TEACHER
SAID.
NOAH LOOKED AT THE PAPER AND EXPLAINED:
"IT'S JUST THAT THE COW ATE ALL THE GRASS AND
AS THERE WAS NO MORE GRASS, THE COW LEFT."

05
APRIL

WHY DID JAMES PUT HIS TEDDY BEAR
IN THE FREEZER?
BECAUSE HE WANTED A POLAR BEAR.

06
APRIL

OLIVER IS IN THE PARK AND JO COMES UP
TO HIM AND SAYS:
"YOU ARE WEARING ONE BROWN AND
ONE BLACK SHOE!!!!!"
AND THE LITTLE BOY REPLIES:
"AND IT'S NO BIG DEAL, AT HOME I'VE
GOT ANOTHER PAIR EXACTLY THE SAME."

07
APRIL

WHAT DID THE PENCIL
SAY TO THE SHARPENER?
STOP GOING IN CIRCLES
AND GET TO THE POINT.

08
APRIL

THE TEACHER AT SCHOOL ASKS:
"HENRY TELL ME A WORD THAT HAS THE
LETTER "O" IN IT MULTIPLE TIMES."
"GOALPOSTS, MISS."
"VERY GOOD, HENRY. NOW YOU, CHLOE."
SHE THINKS AND ANSWERS:
"GOOOOOOOOOOOOOOOOOOOOOOAL"

09
APRIL

CHARLOTTE SAYS TO HER MOTHER:
"DO YOU KNOW WHAT I'M GOING TO BUY
YOU FOR YOUR BIRTHDAY? I'M GOING TO
GIVE YOU A NICE GLASS JAR."
"BUT CHARLOTTE, I ALREADY HAVE A GLASS
JAR," HER MOTHER REPLIES."
"NOT ANYMORE, BECAUSE I JUST BROKE IT."

10
APRIL

A MAN GOES TO THE CIRCUS LOOKING FOR
A JOB AND THE OWNER ASKS HIM:
"WELL, WHAT CAN YOU DO?"
"I CAN IMITATE BIRDS."
"HA, EVERYONE KNOWS HOW TO DO THAT."
"WELL, IN THAT CASE, I'LL BE ON MY WAY."
THEN THE MAN FLEW AWAY..

11
APRIL

WHY DO BIRDS FLY SOUTH?
BECAUSE IT'S TOO FAR TO WALK.

12 APRIL

TWO FRIENDS ARE WALKING DOWN THE STREET AND ONE ASKS THE OTHER:
"WHAT TIME IS IT?"
"IT'S TWELVE O'CLOCK."
"OH, IT'S SO LATE."
"WELL, YOU SHOULD HAVE ASKED ME BEFORE THEN."

13 APRIL

JO WALKS INTO A PHARMACY AND SAYS:
"I WANT SOME GLASSES."
THE PHARMACIST ASKS HER:
"FOR THE SUN?"
AND SHE ANSWERS:
"NOT FOR THE SUN, FOR ME!"

14 APRIL

WHEN THE WAITRESS IN A NEW YORK CITY RESTAURANT BROUGHT AN ENGLISHMAN THE SOUP OF THE DAY, HE WAS CONFUSED AND SAID:
"GOOD HEAVENS, WHAT IS THIS?"
"IT'S BEAN SOUP," SHE REPLIED.
"I DON'T CARE WHAT IT HAS BEEN BEFORE, BUT WHAT IS IT NOW?"

15
APRIL

"MUM, MUM, I GOT A GRADE 9!"
"OH, REALLY? IN WHAT SUBJECT?"
"WELL... A 3 IN MATHS, A 2 IN
ENGLISH, A 2 IN LITERATURE AND
A 2 IN GEOGRAPHY."

16
APRIL

SOPHIE ASKS HER FATHER:
"DADDY, WHAT ARE YOU GOING TO GIVE
ME WHEN I TURN 18?"
THE FATHER POINTS AT COOL RED CAR
PARKED ON THE STREET AND SAYS:
"CAN YOU SEE THAT CAR OVER THERE?"
THE EXCITED LITTLE GIRL REPLIES:
"YES!!!"
HER FATHER THEN SAYS:
"WELL, A T-SHIRT IN THE SAME COLOUR."

17
APRIL

"DAD, WHEN I GROW UP I WANT
TO BE JUST LIKE YOU."
"AND WHY IS THAT, MY SON?"
"SO I CAN HAVE A SON JUST LIKE ME!"

18
APRIL

"DAD, DAD, TELL ME A JOKE!"
"NOT NOW, SON, FIRST YOU'D BETTER HELP ME WASH THE DISHES."
"HA, HA, HA, HA, HA, THAT'S A GOOD ONE!"

19
APRIL

MATT WAS GIVEN A BICYCLE AND WENT OUT TO GIVE IT A TEST RIDE:
"MUM, LOOK, WITHOUT ONE HAND!"
AFTER A FEW MINUTES:
"LOOK, MUM, WITHOUT BOTH HANDS!"
WHEN HE PASSES BY HIS MOTHER AGAIN, HE EXCLAIMS:
"LOOK MUM, NO TEETH!"

20
APRIL

"SAM, PLEASE DON'T KEEP ASKING THE NEIGHBOUR FOR SWEETS."
"BUT I NEVER ASK FOR THEM, AND NOW I KNOW WHERE TO FIND THE SWEETS."

21
APRIL

"OLIVIA, WHAT ARE YOU DOING TAKING A SHOWER WITH AN UMBRELLA?" "DAD, WHAT DO YOU WANT ME TO DO IF WE DON'T HAVE ANY TOWELS?"

22
APRIL

ONCE UPON A TIME A LITTLE FROG WAS BY A LAKE WHEN SUDDENLY IT STARTED TO RAIN, SO THE FROG SAID: "I BETTER GET IN THE WATER, BEFORE I GET WET!"

23
APRIL

WHY WAS SIX AFRAID OF SEVEN? BECAUSE SEVEN, EIGHT, NINE!

24
APRIL

"MUM, IS IT TRUE THAT
BEES MAKE HONEY?"
"YES, THAT'S RIGHT."
"BUT HOW DO THEY
CLOSE THE JAR?"

25
APRIL

WHAT DO BEES USE
TO STYLE THEIR HAIR?
HONEYCOMBS.

26
APRIL

WHAT HAS A NOSE AND
FLIES BUT CAN'T SMELL?
AN AEROPLANE!

27
APRIL

WHY DID THE BUS STOP?
BECAUSE IT SAW A
ZEBRA CROSSING

28
APRIL
WHAT DID THE DOG
SAY TO THE FLEA?
STOP BUGGING ME!

29
APRIL
"DAD, THE MOSQUITOES ARE BITING
ME AND KEEPING ME AWAKE!"
THE BOY'S DAD REPLIES:
"WELL SON, TURN OFF THE LIGHT,
MAYBE THEY'LL GO AWAY."
THE BOY TURNS OFF THE LIGHT WHEN
SUDDENLY A FIREFLY ENTERS HIS
ROOM, AND THE CHILD SHOUTS AGAIN:
"DAD, NOW THEY ARE COMING AFTER
ME WITH A TORCH!"

30
APRIL

THE TEACHER ASKS EVELYN A QUESTION:
"WHAT IS 14 POTATOES DIVIDED BY 7
PEOPLE, EVELYN?"
"MASHED POTATOES, SIR."

01
MAY

WHY DID THE GRANDMA SIT LISTENING
TO MUSIC IN THE ROCKING CHAIR
WITH HER ROLLER BLADES ON?
BECAUSE SHE WANTED TO
ROCK AND ROLL.

02
MAYO

WHAT IS A CAT'S FAVOURITE SONG?
THREE BLIND MICE.

03 MAY

"SIR, HERE IS MY WORK."
"WHAT IS THIS? IT REALLY
LACKS PRESENTATION SKILLS."
"LADIES AND GENTLEMEN, I
PRESENT TO YOU... MY WORK!"

04 MAY

WHY DID OUR DAD START US IN
THE LIFT BUSINESS?
BECAUSE HE THOUGHT IT WAS A
GOOD WAY TO RAISE HIS KIDS.

05 MAY

"MUM, MUM, THE PASTA IS DELICIOUS."
"WELL, YOU CAN SAY THAT AGAIN!"
"MUM, MUM, THE PASTA IS DELICIOUS."

06 MAY

"HONEY, CAN YOU BRING ME THE BABY."
"WAIT UNTIL HE CRIES."
"WAIT UNTIL HE CRIES? BUT WHY?"
"BECAUSE I CAN'T FIND HIM!"

07 MAY

WHAT HAPPENS WHEN YOU
WEAR A WATCH ON A PLANE?
TIME FLIES BY!

08 MAY

WHY DID THE
COW WANT TO BE
ABDUCTED BY SPACE
ALIENS?
IT WANTED TO VISIT
THE MONODON.

09
MAY

WHY WAS THE MOBILE PHONE SCARED TO GO TO THE DENTIST? HE DIDN'T WANT HIM TO TAKE OUT HIS BLUE TOOTH.

10
MAY

WHEN I GOT MYSELF A NEW LADDER, THERE WAS NO NEED TO DO ANY TRAINING. I HAD THE STEP-BY-STEP MANUAL.

11
MAYO

"WHAT DO YOU DO?"
"I'VE BEEN INVENTING THINGS FOR A LONG TIME."
"OH, REALLY? SO, WHAT HAVE YOU INVENTED?"
"SO FAR; WHEELS, LIGHT BULBS, AND THE TELEPHONES..."
"YOU'RE LYING!"
"YOU SEE? I INVENT EVERYTHING."

12
MAY

A MAN WALKS INTO HIS FRIEND'S GARDEN AND SEES A SIGN THAT SAYS "BEWARE OF THE DOG".
SUDDENLY HE SEES A TINY LITTLE DOG AND ASKS HIS FRIEND:
"BUT WHY ARE YOU PUTTING UP THAT SIGN IF THE DOG SEEMS SO HARMLESS?"
"YOU DON'T KNOW HOW MANY TIMES HE'S BEEN STEPPED ON!"

13
MAY

"JAMES, WHY DOES YOUR GEOGRAPHY EXAM HAVE A BIG ZERO OVER IT?"
"IT'S NOT A ZERO, THE TEACHER RAN OUT OF STARS, SO SHE GAVE ME A MOON INSTEAD!"

14
MAY

"WHAT TATTOO SHOULD I GET?"
"THINK OF SOMETHING THAT YOU'LL LOVE FOR THE REST OF YOUR LIFE."
"CROQUETTES!"

15
MAY

MATT'S MUM ASKS HIM:
"HOW COME YOU DIDN'T GET
ME A BIRTHDAY PRESENT?"
MATT LOOKING CONFUSED
REPLIES:
"YOU DID SAY I SHOULD
SURPRISE YOU, RIGHT?"

16
MAY

WHAT MUSIC ARE
BALLOONS SCARED OF?
POP MUSIC!

17
MAY

"WHAT BOTHERS YOU MORE:
IGNORANCE OR INDIFFERENCE?"
"I HAVE NO IDEA, AND I DON'T CARE!"

18 MAY

"TELL ME A WORD THAT BEGINS WITH S."
"YESTERDAY."
"YESTERDAY DOESN'T START WITH S."
"WHAT DO YOU MEAN? YESTERDAY WAS SUNDAY!"

19 MAY

"WOW, CANDLES! WHAT ARE WE CELEBRATING?"
"THAT OUR ELECTRICITY HAS BEEN CUT OFF...."

20 MAY

I ASKED MY BOSS
"WHERE DO YOU WANT THIS BIG ROLL
OF BUBBLE WRAP, SIR?"
"JUST POP IT IN THE CORNER, HE SAID.
IT TOOK ME THREE HOURS."

21
MAY

WHAT DO YOU CALL
MONKEYS WITH BANANAS
IN BOTH OF THEIR EARS?
ANYTHING YOU WANT…
THEY CAN'T HEAR YOU!

22
MAY

TWO FRIENDS MEET IN THE STREET:
"A DOG BIT ME ON THE LEG THE
OTHER DAY."
"DID YOU PUT ANYTHING ON IT?"
"NO, THE DOG LIKED IT JUST THE
WAY IT WAS."

23
MAY

WHAT IS THE DIFFERENCE BETWEEN A
SCHOOL TEACHER AND A TRAIN DRIVER?
A SCHOOL TEACHER TELLS YOU TO SPIT
YOUR GUM OUT, BUT A TRAIN DRIVER
SAYS "CHOO CHOO CHOO"

24
MAY

IN A JOB INTERVIEW:
"YOU'LL START OFF BY EARNING £1,000
AND LATER YOU GET £2,000."
"OH OK, I'LL COME BACK LATER THEN."

25
MAY

DID YOU HEAR ABOUT THE
CLOUD WHO BECAME KING?"
RAINED FOR YEARS.

26
MAY

"DID YOU EVER STOP TO THINK THAT WITH ALL
THIS MONEY YOU SPEND ON FLYING KITES YOU
COULD'VE BOUGHT A MOTORCYCLE ALREADY?"
"OH YEAH? DO YOU FLY KITES?"
"NO, I DON'T!"
"SO WHERE'S YOUR MOTORCYCLE THEN?"

27
MAY

A TEACHER TELLS THE CHILDREN:
"SMART PEOPLE ALWAYS DOUBT, ONLY
FOOLS THINK THEY KNOW EVERYTHING."
"ARE YOU SURE, SIR?"
"OF COURSE I'M SURE!"

28
MAY

"HEY, CAN YOU CALL A JUDGE A 'FOOL'?"
"NO."
"AND CAN YOU CALL A FOOL "MR. JUDGE"?"
"YES, YOU CAN DO THIS."
"THANK YOU, MR. JUDGE"

29
MAY

"WHERE ARE YOU GOING?"
"TO GET THE COMPOST FOR THE STRAWBERRIES."
"BUT WHY DON'T YOU TRY THEM WITH CREAM INSTEAD?"

30 MAY

THE TEACHER ASKS CHARLOTTE:
"IF YOU GOT £20 FROM 5 PEOPLE,
WHAT DO YOU GET?"
CHARLOTTE REPLIES:
"A NEW BIKE."

31 MAY

"ME AND HENRY ARE GOING."
"NO SON, IT'S "HENRY AND I"."
"WHAT? SO I'M NOT GOING NOW?"

01 JUNE

WHAT IS ON THE GROUND AND
ALSO A HUNDRED FEET IN THE AIR?
A CENTIPEDE ON ITS BACK!

02
JUNE

TWO FLEAS LYING ON A DOG ARE MEDITATING AT NIGHT. ONE ASKS THE OTHER:
"DO YOU THINK THERE IS LIFE ON OTHER DOGS TOO?"

03
JUNE

MY DAD HAS BEEN WORKING ON A FOOT-CONTROLLED KEYBOARD.
"TODAY, HE FINALLY FINISHED HIS FIRST PRO-TOE-TYPE."

04
JUNE

WHY WAS THE BOY SITTING ON HIS WATCH? BECAUSE HE WANTED TO BE ON TIME.

05
JUNE

WHAT DID ONE CANDLE SAY
TO THE OTHER AT THE END
OF THE BIRTHDAY PARTY?
I'M FEELING A LITTLE BURNED
OUT AFTER THAT PARTY!

06
JUNE

WHY DID THE GIRL EAT THEIR
HOMEWORK ON THEIR BIRTHDAY?
BECAUSE THE TEACHER SAID IT
WAS A PIECE OF CAKE!

07
JUNE

MATT COMES HOME AND HIS MOTHER
SAYS TO HIM:
"MATT, HOW DID THE TEST GO?"
"WELL, MUM, I'M HAPPY BECAUSE I GOT
THE FIRST QUESTION RIGHT."
"AND WHAT WAS THE FIRST QUESTION?"
"MY FIRST AND LAST NAME."

08
JUNE

"DAD, DO YOU HAVE HOLES IN YOUR SOCKS?"
"NO, SON, I DON'T."
"THEN HOW DID YOU GET YOUR FOOT IN THEM?"

09
JUNE

"JESS, CAN YOU GET OUT OF THE CAR AND
CHECK IF THE INDICATORS ARE WORKING?"
"NOW YES, NOW NO, NOW YES, NOW YES,
NOW NO, NOW YES, NOW NO...."

10
JUNE

A MAN GOES INTO A CAFE:
"EXCUSE ME, HOW MUCH IS
THE ICE TEA?"
"5 POUNDS."
"BUT WAIT, THAT'S PRICEY!"
"NO, SIR, IT'S AN ICE TEA."

11
JUNE

WHERE DO COWS GO ON
SATURDAY NIGHT?
THE MOOOOOOOOOOVIES.

12
JUNE

WHAT TIME IS IT WHEN AN
ELEPHANT STEPS ON A WATCH?
TIME TO BUY ANOTHER WATCH.

13
JUNE

WHAT FAMOUS FOOTBALL PLAYER
ALWAYS LEAVES HIS STUFF LYING
AROUND ON THE FLOOR?
MESSI.

14
JUNE

WHAT DO YOU CALL A DOG MAGICIAN?
A LABRA-CADABRA-DOR.

15
JUNE

THE TEACHER ASKED THOMAS:
"CAN YOU PLEASE USE THE WORDS 'LETTER CARRIER IN A SENTENCE? "
THOMAS REPLIES:
"OF COURSE, MISS. MY DAD SAID THAT AFTER SEEING HOW MANY THINGS MY MOM WAS BRINGING ON HOLIDAY, HE WOULD RATHER LETTER CARRIER OWN LUGGAGE."

16
JUNE

OLIVER ASKS HIS FATHER:
"DADDY, WHERE ARE YOU GOING SO FAST?"
"I NEED TO CATCH THE TRAIN."
"OK, BUT YOU'LL BRING IT BACK LATER, WON'T YOU?"

17
JUNE

WHAT DID ONE GOOSE SAY WHEN IT STOMPED ON ANOTHER'S GOOSE'S FOOT? EX-GOOSE ME!

18
JUNE

MY MUM WAS ASKED WHAT ONE THING WOULD SHE TAKE WITH HER TO A DESERT? SHE REPLIED:
"MY CAR DOOR. THAT WAY, IF I GET HOT, I CAN JUST ROLL MY WINDOW DOWN."

19
JUNE

THE GEOGRAPHY TEACHER ASKS JESS:
"KATE, WHERE IS JAPAN?"
"ON PAGE 77."

20
JUNE

THE TEACHER ASKS CHARLOTTE:
"CHARLOTTE, CAN YOU TELL ME WHAT 10+5 IS?"
"OF COURSE I CAN, MISS. BUT HOW COME YOU DON'T KNOW?"

21 JUNE
HOW DOES A CAMEL GO ACROSS THE DESERT WITHOUT GOING HUNGRY? BECAUSE OF ALL THE SAND-WICHES THERE.

22 JUNE
A MAN ENTERS THE DOCTOR'S OFFICE WITH A DUCK STUCK TO HIS HEAD. THE DOCTOR, SURPRISED AND SHOCKED ASKS:
"BUT WHAT ON EARTH HAS HAPPENED?"
THE DUCK ANSWERS:
"I DON'T KNOW, IT ALL STARTED WITH A LUMP ON MY FOOT."

23
JUNE

A BOY SAYS TO HIS FRIENDS:
"WHEN I GROW UP I'M GOING TO BE AN
ASTRONAUT AND TRAVEL TO MARS."
THE OTHER REPLIES:
"AND I WILL GO TO THE MOON!"
THE THIRD SAYS:
"I'M GOING TO THE SUN!"
"WHAT DO YOU MEAN? YOU WILL GET BURNT!"
"COURSE I WON'T – I'LL GO AT NIGHT!"

24
JUNE

WHAT DID ONE SHOOTING
STAR SAY TO THE OTHER?
PLEASED TO METEOR!

25
JUNE

AT THE BAKERY:
"GOOD MORNING, IS THE BREAD
OUT YET?"
"YES, IT'S OUT."
"SO, WHAT TIME WILL IT BE BACK?"

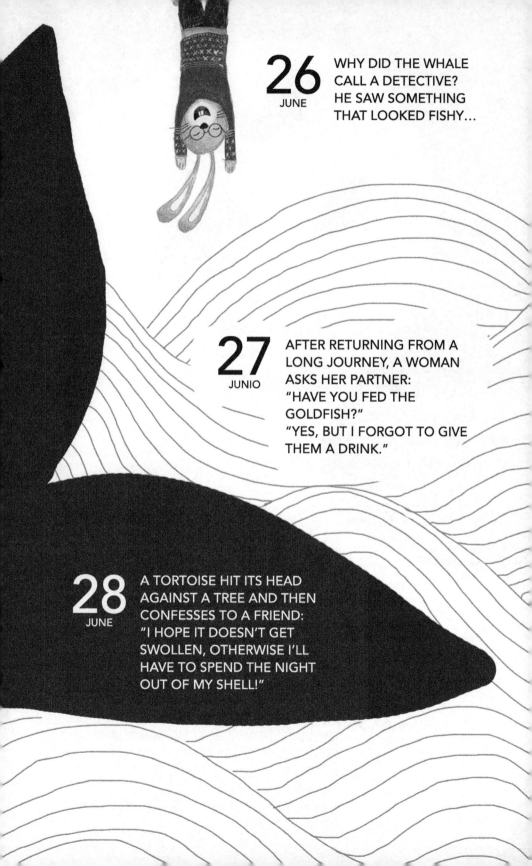

26
JUNE

WHY DID THE WHALE
CALL A DETECTIVE?
HE SAW SOMETHING
THAT LOOKED FISHY...

27
JUNIO

AFTER RETURNING FROM A
LONG JOURNEY, A WOMAN
ASKS HER PARTNER:
"HAVE YOU FED THE
GOLDFISH?"
"YES, BUT I FORGOT TO GIVE
THEM A DRINK."

28
JUNE

A TORTOISE HIT ITS HEAD
AGAINST A TREE AND THEN
CONFESSES TO A FRIEND:
"I HOPE IT DOESN'T GET
SWOLLEN, OTHERWISE I'LL
HAVE TO SPEND THE NIGHT
OUT OF MY SHELL!"

29
JUNE

WHICH WEIGHS MORE, A POUND OF FEATHERS OR A POUND OF BRICKS? ALTHOUGH MOST PEOPLE SAY BRICKS, THEY ARE ACTUALLY THE SAME...

30
JUNE

MATT'S DAD ASKS HIM WHEN HE CAME HOME FROM SCHOOL:
"HI, MATT, HOW WAS SCHOOL TODAY?"
"REALLY GOOD! I LEARNED HOW TO WRITE..."
"SO WHAT DID YOU WRITE?"
"I DON'T KNOW, I HAVEN'T LEARNED HOW TO READ YET!"

01
JULY

"WHAT DOES A GREEN GRAPE
SAY TO A PURPLE ONE?"
"BREATHE! COME ON, BREATHE!"

02
JULY

EMILY ASKED LUKE:
"WHAT DID YOU THINK OF THAT
RESTAURANT ON THE MOON?"
LUKE REPLIED:
"FOOD WAS GOOD, BUT THERE
REALLY WASN'T MUCH ATMOSPHERE."

03
JULY

WHAT'S A GHOST'S
FAVOURITE DESSERT?
I-SCREAM!

04
JULY

WHAT DOES ONE ROCK
SAY TO THE OTHER?
LET'S ROCK AND ROLL!

05
JULY

"SAM, HOW DID YOUR EXAMS GO?"
"JUST LIKE THE NORTH POLE!"
"WHAT DO YOU MEAN?"
"EVERYTHING BELOW ZERO."

06
JULY

WHAT DID THE SEA SAY TO THE
PENGUIN?
NOTHING, IT JUST WAVED.

07
JULY

EVELYN TOLD JESS:
"I'M ON A SEAFOOD DIET."
JESS ASKED:
"DOES THIS MEAN YOU
ONLY EAT FISH?"
"NO, EVERY TIME I SEE
FOOD, I EAT IT!"

08
JULY

WHAT DID ONE TREE SAY TO THE OTHER?
PUT ON YOUR WATERPROOF COAT, A
DOG IS COMING!

09
JULY

WHAT WAS WILLIAM
DOING WITH A POT OF
KETCHUP IN HIS EAR?
LISTENING TO SALSA!

10
JULY

WHAT DID THE SEA SAY TO THE PENGUIN?
NOTHING, IT JUST WAVED.

11
JULY

WHY DID THE SPIDER
TEEN GET IN TROUBLE
WITH HIS MOM?
HE SPENT TOO MUCH
TIME ON THE WEB.

12
JULY

WHY DO PLANTS LIKE TO DISCUSS
ANY ISSUES THEY HAVE?
TO GET TO THE ROOT OF THEIR
PROBLEMS!

13
JULY

"DAD, I JUST SAW A KITTEN WITH ONE EYE."
"WHAT DO YOU MEAN?"
"I PUT MY HAND OVER THE OTHER EYE."

14
JULY

WHAT'S WORSE THAN A
CENTIPEDE WITH SORE FEET?
A GIRAFFE WITH A SORE THROAT!

15
JULY

"BETHANY, BETHANY, WAKE UP LOVE!"
"WHAT'S HAPPENED?"
"YOU FORGOT TO TAKE YOUR
SLEEPING PILLS!...."

16
JULY

OLIVER ENDED UP FAILING HIS
CHAIR EXAM, BUT HE SAID IT
WAS FINE AS HE WAS GOING
TO RESIT IT!

17
JULY

JESS TOLD SAM:
"I HAD SOME FISH LAST NIGHT
THAT HAD A FUNNY TASTE TO IT."
"WHAT WAS IT?"
"NOT SURE, I THINK CLOWNFISH!"

18
JULY

WHY DID THE CHICKEN CROSS THE
ROAD?
TO GET TO THE OTHER SIDE.

19
JULY

AT SCHOOL, THE TEACHER SAYS:
"LET'S DO SOME EXERCISE. LAY DOWN ON YOUR BACK
ON THE FLOOR, LIFT YOUR LEGS AND MOVE THEM AS
IF YOU WERE RIDING A BIKE."
THEY LAY DOWN AND BEGAN TO MOVE THEIR LEGS
IMAGINING THEY WERE RIDING A BIKE. ONLY LILLY
DIDN'T MOVE HER LEGS AT ALL.
"LILLY, WHY AREN'T YOU MOVING YOUR LEGS?"
"BECAUSE I'M GOING DOWNHILL, MISS!"

20
JULY

WHY DID THE BAT CROSS THE ROAD?
BECAUSE IT WAS THE CHICKEN'S DAY OFF.

21
JULY

"DOCTOR, EVERYONE IS LAUGHING AT ME!"
"WELL, THAT'S BECAUSE YOU'RE A CLOWN."

22
JULY

WHAT HAPPENS WHEN YOU TELL A
DUCK A FUNNY JOKE?
THEY QUACK UP.

23
JULY

WANT TO KNOW THE BEST WAY TO BURN 400 CALORIES? LEAVE THE POPCORN IN THE MICROWAVE FOR TOO LONG.

24
JULY

"DAD, MY TEACHER ASKED A QUESTION IN CLASS, AND I WAS THE ONLY ONE WHO PUT MY HAND UP."
"AND WHAT WAS THE QUESTION?"
"WHO HADN'T DONE THEIR HOMEWORK."

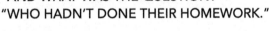

25
JULY

WHAT DID THE BROTHER FOOT SING TO HIS SISTER? HEY SOLE SISTER.

26
JULY

"DO YOU WANT TO HEAR A POPCORN JOKE? "
"NO, SORRY, IT'S TOO CORNY..."

27
JULY

WHAT DID THE MOON ASK
TO THE SUN?
HOW COME YOU'RE SO
BIG AND YET YOU'RE NOT
ALLOWED OUT AT NIGHT?

28
JULY

WHY CAN'T A PERSON'S
NOSE BE 20 INCHES LONG?
BECAUSE THEN IT WOULD
BE A FOOT!

29 JULY

NOAH AND OLIVIA ARRIVE
TO SCHOOL LATE AND THE
TEACHER ASKS THEM:
"NOAH, WHY WERE YOU LATE?"
"I WAS DREAMING THAT I WAS
TRAVELLING ALL OVER THE
WORLD, I VISITED SO MANY
COUNTRIES, SO I WOKE UP A
LITTLE LATE."
"AND YOU, OLIVIA?"
"I WENT TO THE AIRPORT
TO MEET HIM!"

30 JULY

A NEW BOY INTRODUCES HIMSELF TO THE
CLASS:
"GOOD MORNING, I AM JOE KING."
MATT REPLIES:
"SORRY, BUT IT IS THE MORNING, SO
WHAT'S THE JOKE?"

31 JULY

WHY DO SOME
CHILDREN PUT
SUGAR UNDER
THEIR PILLOWS?
TO HAVE SWEET
DREAMS.

01
AUGUST

WHAT DID THE SICK
CHICKEN SAY?
OH NO! I HAVE
THE PEOPLE-POX!

02
AUGUST

WHY WAS THE DUCK NAMED
'CLASS CLOWN'?
HE WAS ALWAYS QUACKIN'
JOKES IN CLASS!

03
AUGUST

DAVID CALL THE SCHOOL:
"HELLO?"
"HELLO? GOOD MORNING!"
"GOOD MORNING! MY SON CAN'T GO TO SCHOOL
TODAY BECAUSE HE IS FEELING UNWELL."
"OH REALLY? BUT WHO AM I TALKING TO NOW THEN?"
"ERM... MY DAD."

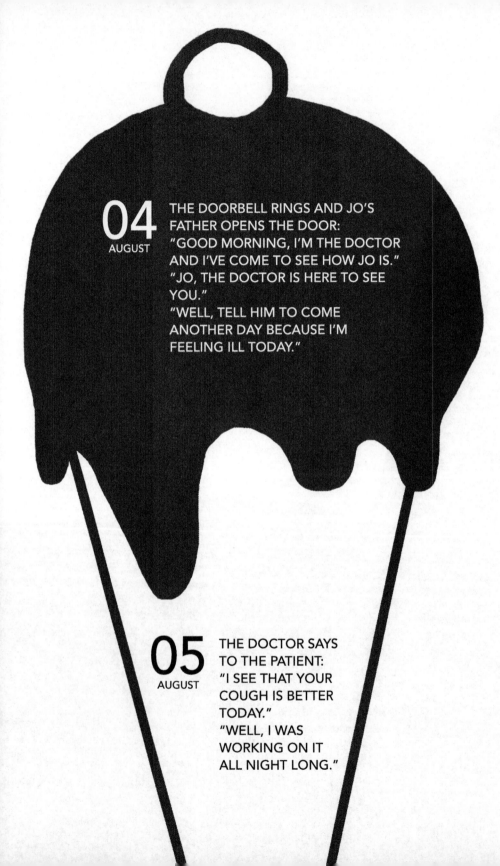

04
AUGUST

THE DOORBELL RINGS AND JO'S FATHER OPENS THE DOOR: "GOOD MORNING, I'M THE DOCTOR AND I'VE COME TO SEE HOW JO IS." "JO, THE DOCTOR IS HERE TO SEE YOU." "WELL, TELL HIM TO COME ANOTHER DAY BECAUSE I'M FEELING ILL TODAY."

05
AUGUST

THE DOCTOR SAYS TO THE PATIENT: "I SEE THAT YOUR COUGH IS BETTER TODAY." "WELL, I WAS WORKING ON IT ALL NIGHT LONG."

06
AUGUST

ONCE UPON A TIME, A CENTIPEDE WAS TAKING A WALK OUTSIDE WHEN SUDDENLY A CHICKEN WANTED TO EAT HIM. HE RAN DESPERATELY TO THE DOOR OF HIS HOUSE AND SHOUTED TO HIS MOTHER:
"MUM, MUM, OPEN THE DOOR, A CHICKEN WANTS TO EAT ME!"
AND HIS MUM ANSWERS:
"I'M COMING! JUST LET ME PUT ON MY SHOES."
"NOOOO"

07
AUGUST

"DOCTOR, DOCTOR, WHEN I TOUCH ME HERE IT HURTS, AND HERE TOO, HERE, HERE, AND HERE...."
THE DOCTOR THEN REPLIES:
"MY FRIEND, THAT'S BECAUSE YOU HAVE IS A BROKEN FINGER."

08
AUGUST

"MUM, MUM, CAN YOU GIVE ME TWO POUNDS FOR THAT POOR MAN WHO IS SHOUTING BY HIMSELF IN THE STREET?"
"YES, JAMES, WHAT A GOOD HEART YOU HAVE! BUT WHAT IS THE MAN SHOUTING ANYWAY?"
"ICE-CREAM FOR TWO POUNDS!"

09
AUGUST

"HEY, WHAT'S YOUR FAVOURITE DISH AND WHY?"
"WELL, BIG AND DEEP ONES BECAUSE THEY CAN FIT MORE FOOD ON THEM...."

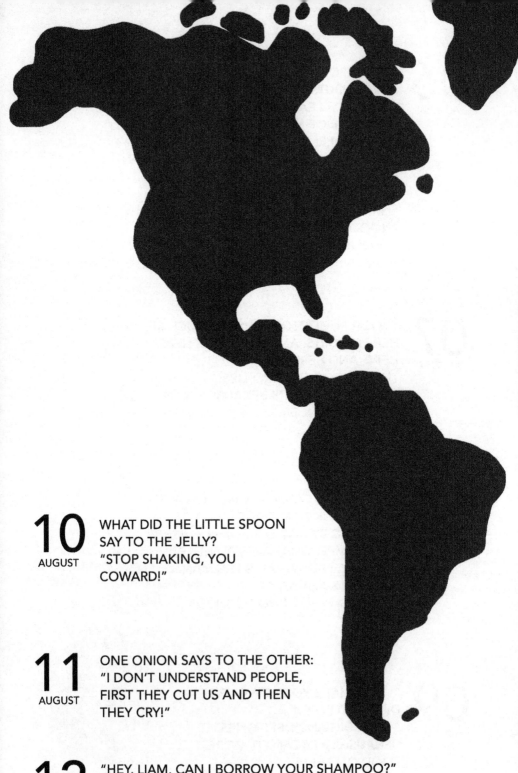

10
AUGUST

WHAT DID THE LITTLE SPOON
SAY TO THE JELLY?
"STOP SHAKING, YOU
COWARD!"

11
AUGUST

ONE ONION SAYS TO THE OTHER:
"I DON'T UNDERSTAND PEOPLE,
FIRST THEY CUT US AND THEN
THEY CRY!"

12
AUGUST

"HEY, LIAM, CAN I BORROW YOUR SHAMPOO?"
"BUT DON'T YOU HAVE YOURS?"
"YES, BUT MINE SAYS IT'S FOR DRY HAIR AND MY
HAIR IS ALREADY WET."

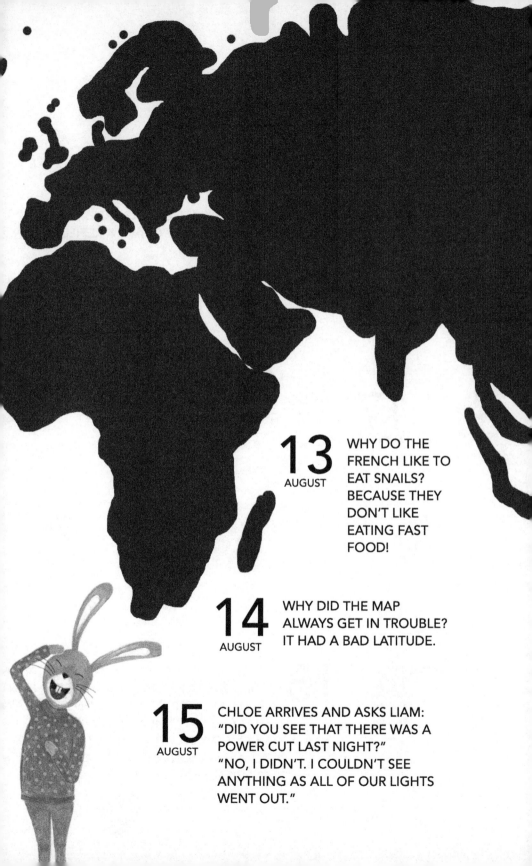

13
AUGUST

WHY DO THE FRENCH LIKE TO EAT SNAILS? BECAUSE THEY DON'T LIKE EATING FAST FOOD!

14
AUGUST

WHY DID THE MAP ALWAYS GET IN TROUBLE? IT HAD A BAD LATITUDE.

15
AUGUST

CHLOE ARRIVES AND ASKS LIAM: "DID YOU SEE THAT THERE WAS A POWER CUT LAST NIGHT?" "NO, I DIDN'T. I COULDN'T SEE ANYTHING AS ALL OF OUR LIGHTS WENT OUT."

16
AUGUST

DAVID WENT TO THE COFFEE SHOP AND ASKED THE BARISTA HOW MUCH A CUP OF COFFEE WAS. THE BARISTA SAID:
"TWO POUNDS AND THE REFILLS ARE FREE."
"GREAT! IN THAT CASE, I'LL JUST HAVE A REFILL THEN."

17
AUGUST

WHY DOESN'T THE SUN GO TO COLLEGE?
BECAUSE IT HAS A MILLION DEGREES!

18
AUGUST

AT THE CINEMA, TWO FRIENDS ARE TALKIN
NONSTOP. THE WOMAN SITTING IN FRONT
OF THEM TURNS AROUND AND COMPLAIN
THAT SHE CAN'T HEAR ANYTHING.
"WHY DO YOU WANT TO LISTEN TO OUR
CONVERSATION ANYWAY?", ONE OF THEM
ANSWERS.

19
AUGUST

TWO FRIENDS ARE WALKING DOWN THE STREET AND ONE SAYS TO THE OTHER: "LOOK, THERE'S A WATCH OVER THERE!" "OH, IT'S MINE. IT'S JUST THAT TIME GETS AWAY FROM ME SOMETIMES."

20
AUGUST

HOW ARE COFFEE BEANS LIKE CHILDREN? THEY'RE ALWAYS GETTING GROUNDED!

21
AUGUST

IN A SPANISH LESSON, THE TEACHER ASKS HER STUDENTS TO WRITE A LETTER AS IF THEY WERE THE PRESIDENT OF THE COUNTRY.
THEY ALL START WORKING, APART FROM SOPHIE.
THE TEACHER IS INTRIGUED AND ASKS HER:
"WHY AREN'T YOU WRITING THE LETTER, SOPHIE?"
"BECAUSE I'M WAITING FOR MY SECRETARY TO ARRIVE."

22
AUGUST

ONE DAY EMILY SAYS TO HER DAD:
"DADDY, DO AVOCADOS HAVE EYES?"
AND HER FATHER SAYS TO HER:
"NO, EMILY."
"OH, I GUESS I JUST ATE A TOAD THEN."

23
AUGUST

OLIVIA ASKS HER MUM:
"WHY DOESN'T MY DAD HAVE MUCH HAIR?"
"BECAUSE YOUR DAD IS VERY SMART."
"SO WHY DO YOU HAVE SO MUCH HAIR THEN?"

24
AUGUST

JAMES WAS SAT AT THE TABLE EATING A SANDWICH
DURING LUNCHTIME. A BOY PASSED BY AND THREW
IT ONTO THE FLOOR.
THE TEACHER, WHO SAW HIM CRYING, ASKED HIM:
"WHY ARE YOU CRYING, JAMES"
"BECAUSE THAT BOY JUST THREW MY SANDWICH
ON THE FLOOR."
THE TEACHER SAYS TO HIM:
"WAS IT ON PURPOSE?"
JAMES, IN TEARS, ANSWERS:
"NO, IT WAS ON THE TABLE."

25
AUGUST

MATT ASKS LILLY:
"WHAT ARE YOU DOING"
"I'M WRITING A LETTER TO MY DOG."
"BUT YOU DON'T EVEN KNOW HOW TO WRITE."
"I KNOW, BUT THAT'S FINE AS MY DOG CAN'T
READ ANYWAY."

26
AUGUST

WHY ARE WITCHES AND HOLIDAYS SO SIMILAR?
BECAUSE THEY BOTH FLY BY!

27
AUGUST

WHAT DID THE SANDWICH
SAY TO THE DOORMAN?
LETTUCE IN.

28
AUGUST

"DO YOU PRAY BEFORE EATING?"
"NO, BECAUSE MY FATHER IS A
GOOD COOK."

29
AUGUST

"CAN FEBRUARY MARCH?"
"NO, BUT APRIL MAY."

30
AUGUST

WILLIAM AND LUCY'S MUM WALKS INTO THE KITCHEN:
"WHO HAS THE CAKE THE CAKE THAT WAS ON KITCHEN SIDE?"
LUCY REPLIES:
"IT WASN'T ME, MUM! WILLIAM ATE IT!"
"NO I DIDN'T!" SAID WILLIAM.
"YES, DO YOU DID!" REPLIED LUCY.
"YOU'RE SUCH A LIAR! YOU WEREN'T EVEN THERE WHEN I WAS EATING IT."

31
AUGUST

DAVE WENT IN TO A PET SHOP AND ASKED THE ASSISTANT:
"CAN I BUY A GOLDFISH?"
THE ASSISTANT REPLIED:
"DO YOU WANT AN AQUARIUM?"
"THE FISH'S STAR SIGN DOESN'T REALLY MATTER", DAVE ANSWERED

01
SEPTEMBER

02
SEPTEMBER

WILLIAM AND OLIVIA WERE TELLING JOKES AND THEN OLIVIA ASKS WILLIAM:
"SHOULD I TELL YOU A JOKE BACKWARDS?"
"OKAY THEN."
"WELL, YOU NEED TO LAUGH FIRST THEN!"

03
SEPTEMBER
HOW DO YOU KNOW CARROTS
ARE GOOD FOR YOUR EYES?
BECAUSE YOU NEVER SEE RABBITS
WEARING GLASSES!

04
SEPTEMBER
WHAT HAPPENS WHEN A GRAPE GETS
RUN OVER CROSSING THE STREET?
A TRAFFIC JAM!

05
SEPTEMBER
"DOCTOR, I THINK I NEED GLASSES."
"I AGREE, BUT I CAN'T HELP YOU.
THIS IS A BANK!"

06
SEPTEMBER

"LET'S SEE, JAMES, TELL ME A WORD THAT USES THE LETTER "I" MORE THAN ONCE."
JAMES THEN ANSWERS:
"BUT MISS, THAT'S VERY DIFFICULT!
"VERY GOOD, JAMES! VERY GOOD!"

07
SEPTEMBER

MATT ASKED HIS DAD:
"DAD, HAVE YOU SEEN MY SUNGLASSES?"
TO WHICH HIS DAD REPLIED:
"NO SON, HAVE YOU SEEN MY DAD GLASSES?"

08
SEPTEMBER

WHY DID TWO 4S SKIP DINNER? BECAUSE THEY ALREADY 8!

09
SEPTEMBER

EMILY'S DAD ASKS HER:
"EMILY, DO YOU THINK YOUR TEACHER KNOWS
THAT I HELP YOU WITH YOUR HOMEWORK?"
AND EMILY SAYS:
"I THINK SO, DAD. SHE TOLD ME TO TELL YOU
THAT YOU SHOULD GO BACK TO SCHOOL."

10
SEPTEMBER

TOM CALLS A RESTAURANT:
"HELLO?"
"HELLO? THIS IS PAUL'S RESTAURANT."
"GOOD EVENING! COULD YOU TELL ME,
DO YOU SERVE LOBSTERS?"
"WE SERVE ANYONE, YOU ARE VERY
WELCOME TO COME."

11
SEPTEMBER

THE TEACHER SAYS TO MIA:
"MIA, TELL ME FIVE THINGS
THAT CONTAIN MILK."
AND MIA REPLIES:
"FIVE COWS, SIR."

12
SEPTEMBER

"WHAT ARE YOU HAVING, SIR?"
"AN OMELETTE, PLEASE."
WHAT IS YOUR PREFERENCE:
FRENCH OR SPANISH?
"IT MAKES NO DIFFERENCE;
I'M NOT GOING TO TALK TO IT."

13
SEPTEMBER

"WAITER, WAITER, WHAT'S WRONG WITH THIS EGG? "
"I DON'T KNOW MADAM, I ONLY LAY THE TABLE."

14
SEPTEMBER

HOW DID THE GARDENER KNOW HIS HERBS WERE FULLY GROWN? IT WAS JUST ABOUT THYME!

15
SEPTEMBER

"DAD, DO YOU HAVE HOLES IN YOUR SOCKS?"
"NO, SON, I DON'T."
"THEN HOW DID YOU GET YOUR FOOT IN THEM?"

16
SEPTEMBER

WHAT SHOULD YOU NEVER PUT IN AN ICE CREAM SUNDAE?
A SPOON

17
SEPTEMBER

DAVID GOES INTO A LAWYER'S OFFICE AND ASKS THE LAWYER:
"EXCUSE ME, HOW MUCH DO YOU CHARGE?"
"I CHARGE £1,000 TO ANSWER THREE QUESTIONS", THE LAWYER REPLIES.
"WOW! THAT'S A BIT EXPENSIVE ISN'T IT?"
"YES. WHAT'S YOUR THIRD QUESTION?"

18
SEPTEMBER

GEORGE ASKS HIS MUM:
"MUM, HOW ARE BABIES BORN?"
AND HIS MOTHER ANSWERS:
"LOOK SON, FIRST THE HEAD
COMES OUT, THEN THE ARMS,
THEN THE BODY, AND FINALLY
THE FEET."
AND GEORGE REPLIES,
"AHHH! SO THEY MAKE THEM IN
PARTS?"

19
SEPTEMBER

"MY DOG HAS EIGHT LEGS!",
THOMAS TELLS LILLY.
"THAT'S IMPOSSIBLE!"
"HONESTLY! HE HAS TWO IN
FRONT AND TWO BEHIND; TWO
ON ONE SIDE AND TWO ON
THE OTHER SIDE."

20
SEPTEMBER

"WHAT ARE YOU WRITING?"
"A LETTER FOR ME."
"AND WHAT IS IN IT?"
"I DON'T KNOW. I
WON'T RECEIVE IT UNTIL
TOMORROW."

21
SEPTEMBER
DO YOU KNOW WHY YOU NEVER SEE ELEPHANTS HIDING UP IN TREES? BECAUSE THEY'RE REALLY GOOD AT IT.

22
SEPTEMBER
WHAT DID THE NOSE SAY TO THE FINGER? STOP TOUCHING ME!

23
SEPTEMBER
WHERE DOES A TURTLE GO WHEN IT'S RAINING? A SHELL-TER!

24
SEPTEMBER

WHAT DOES THE BELL
SAY TO THE FINGER?
IF YOU TOUCH ME, I
WILL START SHOUTING.

25
SEPTEMBER

THE PHONE RINGS:
"HELLO, DO YOU DO
LAUNDRY THERE?"
"NO."
"OH, HOW DISGUSTING!"

26
SEPTEMBER

SOPHIE, WATCHING TV WITH HIS MOTHER, ASKS HER:
"MUM, WHAT LANGUAGE ARE THEY SPEAKING?"
"THEY ARE FROM SPAIN AND THEY SPEAK SPANISH."
"IT'S A GOOD THING I WAS BORN IN ENGLAND!
IF I HAD BEEN BORN IN SPAIN, I WOULDN'T
UNDERSTAND A WORD!"

27
SEPTEMBER

AN EXECUTIVE SAYS TO HER
SECRETARY:
"CAN'T YOU HEAR THE
PHONE RINGING? WHY
AREN'T YOU ANSWERING IT?"
"WHY SHOULD I? ALL OF THE
CALLS ARE FOR YOU".

28
SEPTEMBER

WHAT WAS THE EGG'S
LEAST FAVOURITE DAY
OF THE WEEK?
FRY-DAY!

29
SEPTEMBER

WHAT DO YOU CALL A
BEAR WITH NO TEETH?
A GUMMY BEAR!

30
SEPTEMBER

WHAT DO YOU CALL A
EGG PRANKSTER?
A PRACTICAL YOLKER!

01
OCTOBER

WHY SHOULD YOU
NEVER TRUST STAIRS?
THEY'RE ALWAYS UP
TO SOMETHING.

02
OCTOBER

"DOCTOR, DOCTOR, I
KEEP SEEING DOUBLE!"
"TAKE A SEAT"
"WHICH ONE?"

03
OCTOBER

"KNOCK, KNOCK"
"WHO'S THERE?"
"ICE CREAM"
"ICE CREAM WHO?"
"ICE CREAM IF YOU DON'T
LET ME IN!"

04
OCTOBER

"WHAT IS YOUR BIGGEST FLAW?"
"I GET INVOLVED IN OTHER
PEOPLE'S CONVERSATIONS"
"I WASN'T ASKING YOU, I WAS
ASKING HIM"
"OH, SORRY"

05
OCTOBER

WHAT SEA CREATURES SAY
HELLO SIXTEEN TIMES?
TWO OCTOPUSES
SHAKING HANDS.

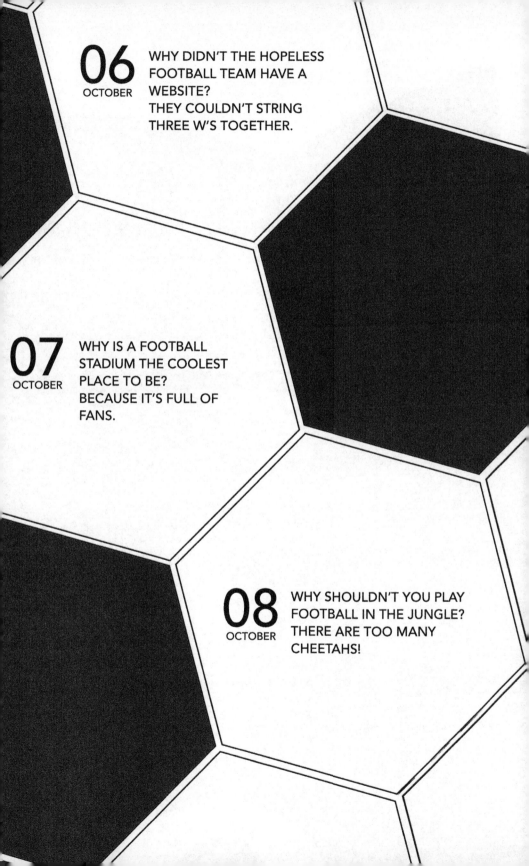

06
OCTOBER

WHY DIDN'T THE HOPELESS
FOOTBALL TEAM HAVE A
WEBSITE?
THEY COULDN'T STRING
THREE W'S TOGETHER.

07
OCTOBER

WHY IS A FOOTBALL
STADIUM THE COOLEST
PLACE TO BE?
BECAUSE IT'S FULL OF
FANS.

08
OCTOBER

WHY SHOULDN'T YOU PLAY
FOOTBALL IN THE JUNGLE?
THERE ARE TOO MANY
CHEETAHS!

09
OCTOBER

THERE WAS A MAN SO CHEAP THAT HE DREAMED HE WAS HAVING A COFFEE IN A RESTAURANT... AND WOKE UP IN ORDER NOT TO PAY FOR IT.

10
OCTOBER

A WAITER SAYS TO A CUSTOMER: "WE HAVE A 9 POUND MENU AND A 6 POUND MEAL." "WHAT'S THE DIFFERENCE?" "3 POUNDS."

11
OCTOBER

WHAT IS THE DIFFERENCE BETWEEN A PIANO AND A FISH? YOU CAN TUNE A PIANO BUT YOU CAN'T TUNA FISH!

12
OCTOBER

"IS THIS YESTERDAY'S BREAD?"
"YES"
"I'D LIKE TODAY'S BREAD!"
"WELL, COME TOMORROW THEN"

13
OCTOBER

WHAT DO YOU CALL A FISH WITH NO EYE?
"FSSSHH"

14
OCTOBER

HOW MANY TICKLES DOES IT TAKE
TO MAKE AN OCTOPUS LAUGH?
TENTACLES.

15
OCTOBER

WHAT MAKES MUSIC ON YOUR HAIR?
A HEADBAND!

16
OCTOBER

WHY IS A SNAKE DIFFICULT TO FOOL?
YOU CAN'T PULL ITS LEG!

17
OCTOBER

"WILL YOU REMEMBER ME IN A YEAR?"
"YES"
"WILL YOU REMEMBER ME IN A MONTH?"
"YES"
"WILL YOU REMEMBER ME IN A WEEK?"
"YES"
"WILL YOU REMEMBER ME IN A DAY?"
"YES"
KNOCK, KNOCK.
"WHO'S THERE?"
"SEE, YOU FORGOT ME ALREADY!"

18
OCTOBER

WHAT DID THE HAIRBRUSH
SAY TO ITS FRIEND?
MY FRIEND, CAN YOU
COMB OVER HAIR?

19
OCTOBER

A MAN SAYS TO MATT:
-IF YOU GUESS HOW MANY
CHICKENS I HAVE, I'LL GIVE
YOU ALL THREE.

20
OCTOBER

"MUM, MUM! HOW WAS I BORN?"
"THE STORK BROUGHT YOU."
"AND MY SISTER?"
"THEY FOUND HER IN A CABBAGE PATCH"
"WELL, WELL! HASN'T THERE BEEN A
NORMAL BIRTH IN THIS FAMILY!?"

21
OCTOBER

COFFEE IS THE SILENT VICTIM IN OUR HOUSE... IT GETS MUGGED EVERY DAY!

22
OCTOBER

A MAN CLIMBS A TREE AND A POLICEMAN SEES HIM AND SAYS TO HIM:
"YOU! GET DOWN FROM THERE!"
"NO, I CAME HERE TO EAT FIGS...."
"BUT THAT'S AN APPLE TREE!"
"THIS DOESN'T MATTER, I'VE BROUGHT FIGS WITH ME...."

23
OCTOBER

"HEY, DON'T YOU THINK IT'S STRANGE THAT THE HORSE ASKED YOU FOR JUICE?" !YES, IT IS. THAT HORSE NORMALLY ASKS FOR WATER."

24
OCTOBER

WHAT DID THE COFFEE SAY TO THE SUGAR? "MY LIFE WOULD BE BITTER WITHOUT YOU."

25
OCTOBER

WHY WAS THE INSTANT CUP OF COFFEE SO RUDE? HE HAD NO FILTER.

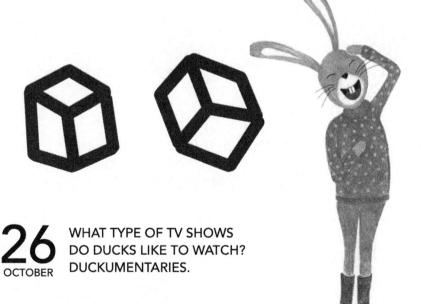

26
OCTOBER

WHAT TYPE OF TV SHOWS DO DUCKS LIKE TO WATCH? DUCKUMENTARIES.

27
OCTOBER

WHAT TIME IS IT WHEN THE
CLOCK STRIKES 13?
TIME TO GET A NEW CLOCK!

28
OCTOBER

HOW DO YOU KNOW WHEN THE
MOON HAS ENOUGH TO EAT?
WHEN IT'S FULL!

29
OCTOBER

WHAT DO COWS SAY WHEN
THEY HEAR A BAD JOKE?
I AM NOT AMOOSED.

30 OCTOBER

DID YOU HEAR ABOUT THE BED BUGS WHO FELL IN LOVE?
THEY'RE GETTING MARRIED IN THE SPRING!

31 OCTOBER

"DEAR, DID YOU CHANGE THE WATER IN THE TANK?"
"NO, THEY HAVEN'T DRUNK LAST WEEK'S WATER YET."

01 NOVEMBER

HOW DO YOU START
AN INSECT RACE?
ONE, TWO, FLEA - GO!

02
NOVEMBER

MATT WALKS INTO THE CINEMA AND FINDS HIS FRIEND SITTING THERE WITH HIS DOG WATCHING THE MOVIE.
THE PET ENJOYS EVERY SCENE SO MATT SAYS:
"IT'S AMAZING: YOUR DOG IS WATCHING AND ENJOYING THE MOVIE!"
THE DOG'S OWNER REPLIES:
"I AM EVEN MORE AMAZED, AS WHEN HE READ THE BOOK HE DIDN'T LIKE IT AT ALL!".

03
NOVEMBER

THE TEACHER ASKS CHARLOTTE:
"WHO DO YOU THINK IS SMARTER: PEOPLE OR PETS?"
CHARLOTTE RESPONDS:
"DOGS."
"HMM OKAY, WHY DO YOU SAY THAT?"
CHARLOTTE ANSWERS:
"WHEN I SAY SOMETHING TO MY DOG, HE UNDERSTANDS EVERYTHING, BUT WHEN HE TALKS TO ME I DON'T UNDERSTAND ANYTHING!"

04
NOVEMBER

WHY DID THE TEACHER PUT ON SUNGLASSES? BECAUSE HER STUDENTS WERE SO BRIGHT!

05
NOVEMBER

HOW DOES THE MOON CUT HIS HAIR?
ECLIPSE IT!

06
NOVEMBER

HOW FAR CAN YOU SEE ON A
CLEAR DAY?
150 MILLION KILOMETRES AWAY,
FROM HERE TO THE SUN!

07
NOVEMBER

WHAT DID ONE PLATE
SAY TO THE OTHER?
DINNER IS ON ME!

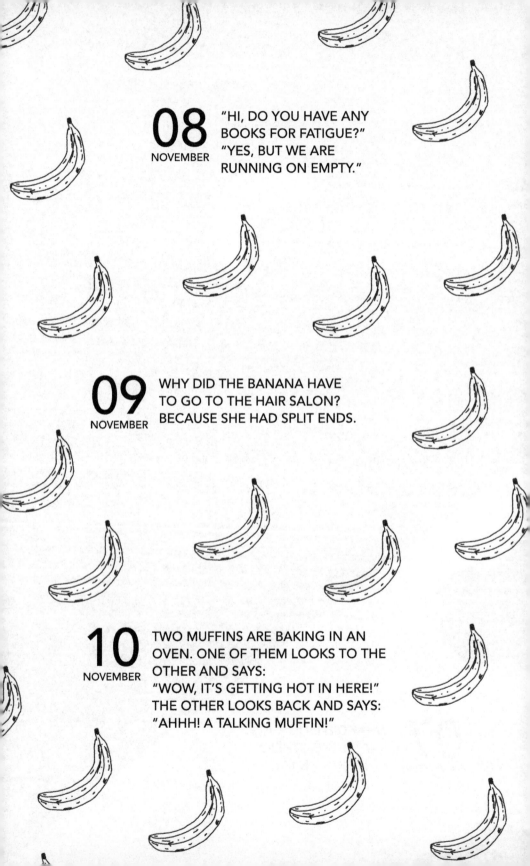

08
NOVEMBER

"HI, DO YOU HAVE ANY BOOKS FOR FATIGUE?"
"YES, BUT WE ARE RUNNING ON EMPTY."

09
NOVEMBER

WHY DID THE BANANA HAVE TO GO TO THE HAIR SALON? BECAUSE SHE HAD SPLIT ENDS.

10
NOVEMBER

TWO MUFFINS ARE BAKING IN AN OVEN. ONE OF THEM LOOKS TO THE OTHER AND SAYS:
"WOW, IT'S GETTING HOT IN HERE!"
THE OTHER LOOKS BACK AND SAYS:
"AHHH! A TALKING MUFFIN!"

11
NOVEMBER

ONE MAN TO THE OTHER:
"EXCUSE ME, YOU HAVE A
BANANA IN YOUR EAR! "
THE OTHER SAYS:
"SORRY, I CAN'T HEAR YOU, I
HAVE A BANANA IN MY EAR!"

12
NOVEMBER

WHAT'S WORSE THAN
FINDING A WORM AFTER
BITING INTO AN APPLE?
FINDING ONLY HALF
THE WORM!

13
NOVEMBER

"DOCTOR, I HAD AN ACCIDENT
AND MY LEGS HURT SO MUCH
THAT I CAN'T WALK."
"LET ME SEE."
TEN MINUTES LATER:
"WELL, IN A WEEK'S TIME
YOU'LL BE WORKING AGAIN."
"DOCTOR, YOU'RE GREAT! NOT
ONLY DO YOU CURE ME, BUT
YOU ALSO FIND ME A JOB!"

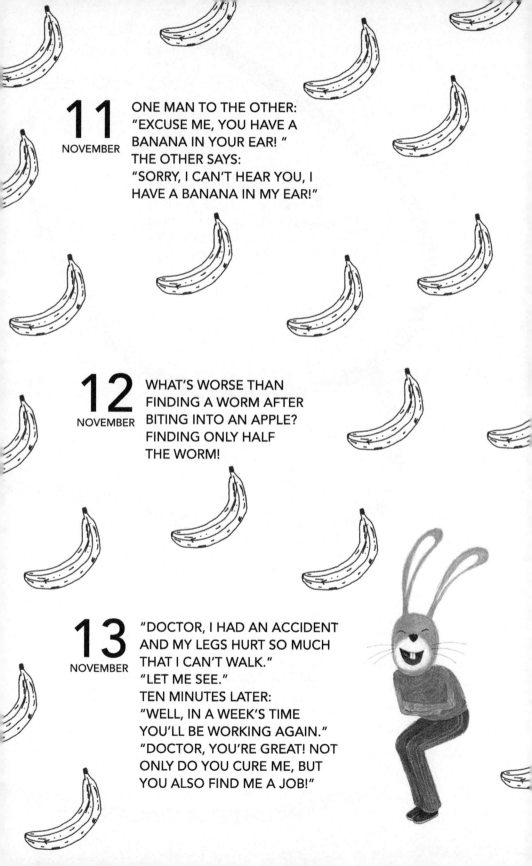

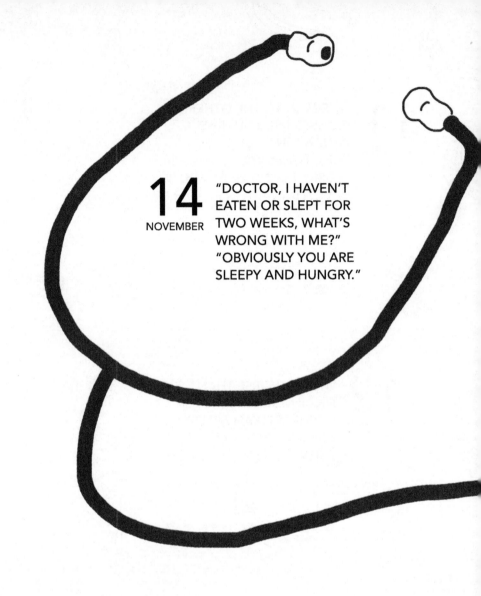

14
NOVEMBER

"DOCTOR, I HAVEN'T EATEN OR SLEPT FOR TWO WEEKS, WHAT'S WRONG WITH ME?" "OBVIOUSLY YOU ARE SLEEPY AND HUNGRY."

15
NOVEMBER

"DOCTOR, DOCTOR, I SEE PINK ELEPHANTS EVERYWHERE." "HAVE YOU SEEN A PSYCHOLOGIST AT ALL?" "NO, DOCTOR, ONLY PINK ELEPHANTS."

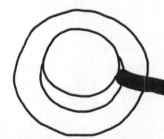

16
NOVEMBER

WHEN DO DOCTORS GET MAD?
WHEN THEY RUN OUT OF PATIENTS!

17
NOVEMBER

A VETERINARIAN GOES TO SEE A DOCTOR.
THE DOCTOR SAYS TO HIM:
"OKAY, TELL ME, WHAT'S THE MATTER WITH YOU?"
AND THE VETERINARIAN REPLIES:
"AH, IF I TELL YOU STRAIGHT AWAY IT'S TOO EASY!"

18
NOVEMBER

"DOCTOR, I CAN'T REMEMBER
ANYTHING LATELY."
"AND HOW LONG HAVE YOU
HAD THIS PROBLEM?"
"WHAT PROBLEM?"

19
NOVEMBER

"DOCTOR, I KEEP
HEARING A RINGING
SOUND."
"THEN YOU SHOULD
PROBABLY ANSWER
THE PHONE!"

20
NOVEMBER

CHLOE GETS UP AND SAYS TO HER DAD:
"DADDY, DADDY, TODAY I WOKE UP
FEELING EAGER TO WORK."
HER DAD REPLIES:
"SO WHAT ARE YOU GOING TO DO?"
"I'M GOING TO GO TO BED TO GET RID
OF THIS FEELING."

21
NOVEMBER

WHAT DID THE FLAME SAY TO HER
FRIENDS AFTER SHE FELL IN LOVE?
I FOUND THE PERFECT MATCH!

22
NOVEMBER

JO'S MUM IS FRYING A LOT OF MUSHROOMS
IN A FRYING PAN AND JO SAYS:
"DOESN'T LOOK LIKE YOU HAVE
MUSHROOM LEFT IN THERE!"

23
NOVIEMBRE

JAMES COMES HOME AND SHOWS HIS MOTHER 100 POUNDS THAT HE FOUND. "JAMES, ARE YOU SURE SOMEONE HASN'T LOST THEM?"
"I'M SURE THEY HAVE, MUM! I EVEN SAW THE MAN WHO WAS LOOKING FOR THEM!"

24
NOVEMBER

"ARE CANDLES HAPPY OR SAD WHEN YOU PUT THEM OUT?"
"NEITHER, THEY'RE DE-LIGHTED."

25
NOVEMBER

"WHY DID THE CHAP THROW THE CONTENTS OF HIS FRIDGE OUT OF THE WINDOW?"
"HE WANTED TO SEE THE BUTTERFLY."

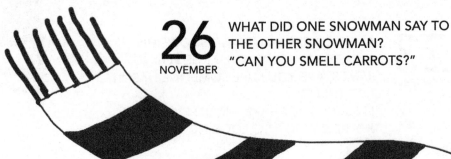

26
NOVEMBER

WHAT DID ONE SNOWMAN SAY TO THE OTHER SNOWMAN? "CAN YOU SMELL CARROTS?"

27
NOVEMBER

JO BRAGS TO HENRY: "DID YOU KNOW THAT WHEN I WAS NINE MONTHS OLD I WAS ALREADY WALKING, I'M VERY INTELLIGENT!" "OH, AND YOU CALL THAT CLEVER? WHEN I WAS THREE YEARS OLD, I WAS STILL BEING CARRIED AROUND!"

28
NOVEMBER

"MATT, CAN YOU GIVE ME AN EXAMPLE OF UNFAIRNESS?" "YES, WHEN MY DAD DOES A REALLY BAD JOB OF MY HOMEWORK, BUT I THEN GET THE BAD MARK."

29
NOVEMBER

"MUM, MUM! DOES A BOTTLE OF INDIAN INK COST A LOT OF MONEY?"
"NO, IT'S CHEAP. WHY'S THAT?"
"THAT'S GOOD THEN! BECAUSE I SPILLED A BOTTLE OF INDINA INK ON YOUR NEW DRESS."

30
NOVEMBER

"YOU SEE DAISY, THERE ARE TWO MAGIC WORDS THAT WILL OPEN MANY DOORS FOR YOU: PULL AND PUSH."

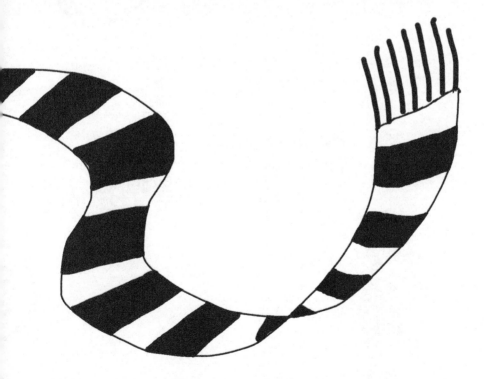

01
DECEMBER

WHEN GEESE ARE AFRAID, DO THEY GET GOOSE BUMPS?

02
DECEMBER

IN A RESTAURANT, A MAN ASKS THE WAIT:
-"EXCUSE ME, DOES THE FISH COME BY ITSELF?"
"NO, SIR. I'LL BRING IT TO YOU."

03
DECEMBER

WHY DON'T COWS HAVE ANY MONEY? BECAUSE FARMERS MILK THEM DRY.

04
DECEMBER

"DOCTOR, DOCTOR! I'VE GOT BROCCOLI GROWING IN MY EAR!"
"IT LOOKS LIKE YOU'RE NOT EATING PROPERLY."

05
DECEMBER

WHERE DO FROGS
DEPOSIT THEIR MONEY?
AT A RIVER-BANK!

06
DECEMBER

JO TOLD NOAH:
"YOU SHOULDN'T WORK OUT NEXT TO THE WATER."
"WHY?"
"YOU MIGHT PULL A "MUSSEL"."

07
DECEMBER

WHY DO
HUMMINGBIRDS HUM?
BECAUSE THEY DON'T
KNOW THE WORDS!

08
DECEMBER

WHAT DID THE EGG SAY
TO THE FRYING PAN?
YOU CRACK ME UP!

09
DECEMBER

WHAT DOES ONE PRINTER
SAY TO ANOTHER PRINTER?
IS THIS SHEET YOURS OR IS IT
MY IMPRESSION?

10
DECEMBER

WHAT DID ONE EYE SAY TO
THE OTHER EYE?
BETWEEN YOU AND I,
SOMETHING SMELLS.

11
DECEMBER

WHAT DID THE TRIANGLE
SAY TO THE CIRCLE?
YOU'RE POINTLESS!

12
DECEMBER

JAMES WENT AND SAID TO
HIS FATHER:
"DAD, I WANT TO MARRY MY
GRANDMOTHER."
AND HIS FATHER REPLIED:
"HOW ARE YOU GOING TO
MARRY MY MOTHER?"
THE BOY ANSWERED:
"BUT YOU MARRIED MY
MOTHER AND I DIDN'T SAY
ANYTHING TO YOU!"

13
DECEMBER

WHAT HAPPENS IF YOU CROSS POISON
IVY WITH A FOUR-LEAF CLOVER?
YOU GET A RASH OF GOOD LUCK!

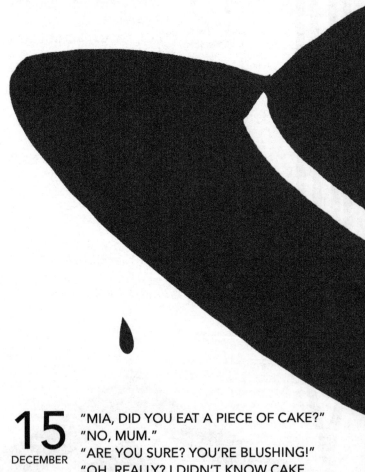

14 DECEMBER

EMILY GETS LOST IN A MUSEUM AND ASKS A SECURITY GUARD: "SIR, HAVE YOU SEEN A LADY THAT IS WITHOUT A LITTLE GIRL LIKE ME?"

15 DECEMBER

"MIA, DID YOU EAT A PIECE OF CAKE?"
"NO, MUM."
"ARE YOU SURE? YOU'RE BLUSHING!"
"OH, REALLY? I DIDN'T KNOW CAKE COULD MAKE YOU BLUSH!"

16 DECEMBER

WHY ARE HAT JOKES THE HARDEST TO UNDERSTAND? BECAUSE THEY ALWAYS GO RIGHT OVER YOUR HEAD!

17
DECEMBER

LILLY COMES TO SCHOOL CRYING
AND THE TEACHER ASKS HIM:
"WHAT'S WRONG LILLY?"
"I GOT ROBBED, TEACHER!"
"OH, MY GOODNESS! WHAT WAS
TAKEN FROM YOU?"
"MY HOMEWORK..."

18
DECEMBER

"I JUST BOUGHT A NEW
HAT WITH A BUILT-IN FAN
THAT KEEPS MY HEAD COOL
DURING HOT WEATHER. IT
REALLY BLOWS MY MIND!"

19
DECEMBER

WHAT DID ONE TOILET SAY TO THE OTHER?
YOU LOOK A BIT FLUSHED.

20
DECEMBER

LIAM AND OLIVIA ARE PLAYING UNTIL THE GIRL
SHOWS HIM HER CLENCHED FIST AND SAYS:
"HEY, CAN YOU GUESS WHAT'S IN MY HAND?"
"HMMM... AN ELEPHANT?"
OLIVIA LOOKS ANNOYED AND REPLIES:
"YEAH, BUT WHAT COLOUR THEN?"

21
DECEMBER

WHAT DID THE
DOCTOR SAY TO
THE ANGRY ADVENT
CALENDAR?
SORRY, BUT
YOUR DAYS ARE
NUMBERED!

22
DECEMBER

"MIA, I'M TOLD YOU'RE VERY
QUICK WITH MATHS. LET'S
SEE, WHAT IS 47 TIMES 126?"
"328!!"
"NOPE! YOU DIDN'T EVEN
COME CLOSE!!!"
"BUT YOU CAN'T TELL ME
THAT I WASN'T FAST..."

23
DECEMBER

CHARLOTTE IS ON THE PLANE AND A FLIGHT ATTENDANT HANDS OUT CHEWING GUM.
"WHAT DO WE NEED THIS FOR?"
"SO THAT YOUR EARS DON'T HURT DURING PRESSURE CHANGES."
WHEN THEY LAND, CHARLOTTE ASKS THE STEWARD:
"SO HOW DO I GET THE GUM OUT OF MY EARS NOW THEN?"

24
DECEMBER

JESS AND MATT ARE SETTING UP THE CHRISTMAS TREE AND MATT SAYS TO JESS:
"LET ME KNOW WHEN THE LIGHTS ARE ON."
AND JESS REPLIES:
"THEY'RE ON... OFF... ON... OFF... ON... OFF..."

25
DECEMBER

TWO DOGS WERE UNDER THE CHRISTMAS TREE AT HOME AND ONE SAID TO THE OTHER:
"FINALLY, THE BATHROOM LIGHTS ARE COMING ON! "

26
DECEMBER

WHAT WOULD YOU GET WHEN YOU CROSSED AN ANGRY SHEEP WITH A GRUMPY COW?
AN ANIMAL IN A BAAAAAAAAD MOOOOOOOD.

27
DECEMBER

THE POLICE ARRIVE AT JAMES' HOUSE...
"POLICE! JAMES, OPEN UP, WE KNOW YOU'RE THERE!"
"WHAT DO YOU WANT?"
"WE JUST WANT TO TALK. OPEN UP."
"HOW MANY OF YOU ARE THERE?"
"SIX."
"WELL, TALK AMONG YOURSELVES THEN!

28
DECEMBER

"WHY DON'T YOU WORK?"
" BECAUSE I'M CRAZY."
"YES, BUT OTHER CRAZY PEOPLE WORK...."
"YEAH, BUT I'M NOT THAT CRAZY!"

29
DECEMBER

THERE IS A LOUD NOISE OF DISHES BREAKING IN THE KITCHEN:
"MIA, WHAT'S HAPPENED? DON'T TELL ME IT'S MORE DISHES..."
"NO MUM, LESS ACTUALLY."

30
DECEMBER

WHAT KIND OF SPORTS CAR DOES A SHEEP LIKE TO DRIVE?
A LAMBORGHINI.

31
DECEMBER

WHY SHOULD YOU PUT YOUR CALENDAR IN THE FREEZER? TO START OFF THE NEW YEAR IN THE COOLEST WAY!

I'M SURE YOU KNOW MORE JOKES!

WRITE THEM IN THE FOLLOWING PAGES

THE END

Printed in Great Britain
by Amazon

39591595R00076